I Can

by Sascha Goddard

OXFORD
UNIVERSITY PRESS
AUSTRALIA & NEW ZEALAND

She gets a big bed.

I can set it up.

He fell in the mud.

I will get him up.

She is on a big run.

I yell not to quit.

He is sad.

I will hug him.

He is hot in the jacket.

I fix the zip.

The dog yaps.

I can pat the dog.

She tips the liquid.
It fizzes.

I am quick.

I mop up the mess.

I can fix it.